WORDS I NEVER SAID

Words I Never Said

Poems From My Heart

Bernie Crawford

To order additional copies of this book, contact:
Xlibris Corporation
1-888-795-4274
www.Xlibris.com
Orders@Xlibris.com
55919

Dedicated to My Wonderful and Beautiful wife of 47 years,
Brenda S. Crawford

My 2 Beautiful and Fantastic daughters,
LaDeadre S. Schanick and Melissa A Griggs

My 3 Outstanding and Lovely Grandchildren,
Gregrey V. Schanick,
Alexis C. Griggs
and Landon D. Griggs

My 2 Great and Faithful Son-in-Laws,
Jeffery V. Schanick and Kevin D. Griggs

Most of all to my Wonderful Savior Jesus Christ.

CONTENTS

INTRODUCTION

I have been writing for a long time, but this is my first publication.
My background is very unique; I was a cotton farmer in northeast Arkansas, where
there's not much opportunity for success, just hard work.

I realized that if I were to have success, I would have to make it myself.
So later on in life I became a professional wrestler in the
National Wrestling Alliance.
From that I realized a higher calling was upon me, so I
committed my life to Jesus Christ, became a minister and
pastor, and founded two churches in my thirty-eight years of ministering.

ZECHARIAH DAVID GRAY

Born 07/23/04   Died 04/18/07

I don't know how to tell you this
I miss you so, Mom and Dad
but I sure did enjoy
what time on earth I had.

I want to tell you both
don't blame yourselves it's okay
Jesus just pulled another flower
for the master's bouquet.

I used to love cars and trucks
and all the things we do
I'd grab your hand, Daddy, and say let's run
oh, I want to tell you, Daddy, I am running the aisles here too.

I'd used to sing in the children's choir
I would see the sparkle in yours and Momma's eyes
you're sitting their right now a thinkin'
God in heaven why.

The truth of the matter is
we all have only a short time on earth
some before others
in a short time live their worth.

I loved Momma's tender hands
when she held me, I was excited through and through
oh yes, before I forget it
tell my brothers I loved them too.

Mom, when I first got here
so much beauty I was in awe
I ran to where there was a lot of people
and there I saw Grandma and Grandpa.

Mom, you and Dad are wandering
to get through this you can't see a way
look at it like this
you got more to go to heaven for than you did yesterday.

Momma keeps on praising Jesus
Dad keeps running them aisles
every time you do
I'll look down with a big ole smile.

Dad, Mom, brothers, and church family
for your pain I'll go over and ask Jesus to pray
remember I'll see you all up here
p.s. hurry with love, Zechariah Gray.

This poem is a contribution to a little man I was blessed to know.
His life was taken so swiftly that no one could understand, especially
his dad and his mom.
All will miss him here on earth; the earth will be a less joyful
place without him, but heaven will be a more exciting place
to go so we can see Zechariah (Will Parker) again.

To all the lingering questions about his sudden removal from
among us, I refer you to an old hymnal. We will understand it
better by and by.
God bless the Gray family, and may you heal from your loss.

A BLOWN KISS

I blew you a kiss today
sent it by air
it came back to me
'cause no one was there.
I'll send it again tomorrow
in hopes you will receive
I hope you hadn't led me on
and I am the one deceived.
I've loved you for a long time
just wanted you to know
if you want take my airmail kiss
then I'll let you go.
I can't take the pressure
I am pulling out my hair
me being here
and you being there.
You sent my kiss back, return to sender
because you love another man
you quit taking my kiss
when you let him put a ring on your hand.

A Broken Bridge

A broken bridge
a thing gone wrong
a soul lost
a family left alone.
Whether it's a love gone bad
or a dream shattered
it always leaves someone
torn and tattered.
When someone you love
leaves home today
darling I love you
are the words to say.
The bridge they are crossing
may break apart
they go soaring with angels
leaving you with a broken heart.
In this thing called life
there is a bridge for all to cross
travel as careful as you can
if it is built well you won't be lost.

A Broken Man

I was a broken man
a scarred and empty soul
down to my last chance
I thought my life was on a roll.
One day I had everything
next day I lost it all
never thought this would happen
thought I'd never fall.
But life can be so uncertain
deals you a hand you can't play
it'll leave you confused and lonely
can't tell night from day.
I can't dream myself into a better life
I have to help myself
I can make it back to the top
if I'll focus on what's left.
Nothing is easier than saying words
and living them day by day
courage is being scarred to death
but saddling up anyway.

A FARMER'S LIFE

A farmer's life is a rough road to hoe
if it's not in your heart
don't plant the first roe.
If you decide to stay
and farm the land
you'll need a strong back
a pair of big hands.
Till the land make the roes straight
get up early
stay up late.
Hip the roes, put the seed in the ground
wait for nature
to bring the rain down.
Daily they work
from sunup to sundown
in the fall they get ready
to harvest the crop from the ground.

A Simple Tear

Enraged by emotions
weeping and crying for days
you shed the sacred tear
sustained only as you pray.
To some you weep at trifles
or fictitious sorrows that draw you near
to others it's your imagination
to you it draws the simple tear.
Driven by grief that comes upon you
sometimes days without end
then by being patient
transform foes to friends.
We face adversity
while others seem to cheer
the only solace we seem to get
is when we shed a simple tear.
If we are persistent in pressing
doubters will gaze and cheer
you will have won the battle for now
by the power of a simple tear.

A simple tear is channeled through the tear duct,
not only to keep it open, but releases emotion from the soul.
It takes a real man or woman to shed a tear,
so weep when you can and never apologize.

Psalm 30:5
For his anger endureth for a moment; in his favor is life: weeping
may endure for a night,
but joy cometh in the morning.

A WANDERING MAN

I am heading down a one-way road
carrying a heavy load
I don't know tomorrow what I'll do.
I am just a wandering man
traveling o're a desert land
I need someone to help me through.
I've bore this pain long enough
drank from defeat's bitter cup
while stumbling along this earthly sod.
Then one day I saw the light
on my Demascus road bright
there I met the son of God.
Now I have a story to tell
I found the Savior in a hotel
on those silk sheets in between.
I am still walking that same old road
I am not carrying the same old load
I found the son of God in john three sixteen.

To not know where
will reveal that you may not
be in control.
To have no sense of direction or a place to
call home can put a man on a course of
loneliness and failure.

Hebrews 13:5
Let your conversation be without covetousness;
and be content with such things as you have:
for he hath said, I will never leave thee,
nor forsake thee.

ALMOST

Almost nearly
not quite plumb
almost smart
is almost dumb.
Almost there
is sometimes between
almost being there
is never being seen.
Almost somewhere
is sometimes here
almost in love
is not always having her near.
Almost happy
is sometimes sad
almost
is never being glad.
You can't be almost
at anything you do
if you're almost
you are never you.

To have it in sight and reach and still not have it is torture.
When we can't have what we see,
our self, will, and ego are worthless.

Acts 26:28
Then Agrippa said unto Paul, "Almost thou pursuedest me to be a
Christian."

Are You almost or altogether.
You alone must Decide.

BEAUTY

What is beauty
I ask you now
is it exterior features
that make you say wow?
Is it a blink of an eye
or the sway of a hip
long swaying hair
or rosy red lip?
What is real beauty
give me your side
I think it is certain qualities
down deep that abide.
From the beginning of life
they are vague and dim
but arise and stand out
as you cultivate them.
To mold to perfection
for all to see
you have become beauty
as you reflect the one you are to be.

I find beauty to be not altogether exterior features, but molded character,
brought about by positive choices, remember while making choices,
choices are making you.

Psalms 149:4
For the LORD taketh pleasure in his people:
he will beautify the meek with salvation.

BEST FRIENDS

You and I are best friends
we vowed to be to the end
and never have anything to mend.
I found that to be true
in everything we do
you chose me over you.
We shared our heartbreaks
when we made some mistakes
vowed to keep each other straight.
Best friends are friends no matter what
it doesn't matter what you got
or if I have not.
I'll stick with you through thick and thin
and will be to you a best friend
as you have since we began.
So thanks for being there
showing me a true friends care
and all we have to each other share.

Someone you can tell everything is your best friend.
A best friend is there when family is nowhere around.
Best friends are molded to you by adversity and the good.
If you are that person, be the best friend you can be,
you may be mine.

Proverb 18:24
A man that hath friends must show himself friendly:
and there is a friend that sticketh closer
than a brother.
JESUS

CAN'T DREAM YOURSELF INTO

You can't dream yourself into a character
nor can you wish yourself rich
everything you can put your hand to
is sewn into life stitch by stitch.
You can't dream yourself into a new home
you have to build it with money and plans
when the building is complete and livable
you see what you did with your hands.
It would be nice to twist your nose
as the story of the genie can do
and have everything at your fingertips
believe that and you are the one fooled
You can have anything you want
have to get it by the sweat of your brow
I am not talking of a make-believe world
but how it is now.

*You can't wiggle your nose like the tale of the genie
and get what you want.
Dreams are good until you put legs on your dreams,
they are only unreachable dreams
Every act you do will bring you closer to your dreams or farther
away.*

*Romans 10:17
So then Faith cometh by hearing,
and hearing by the word of God.*

CHANGING OF TIMES

The changing of time
comes to one and all
you can tell by the pictures
placed on a wall.
Whether we like it or not
that's the way it is
life is like an Alka-Seltzer
that loses its fizz.
Time goes on
and changes too
accept the hand of fate
as it takes you through.
The process of life
each stage and each door
the ticking of the clock
you'll change the more.
When the process is over
you'll have no doubt
you don't look the same
as you did when you started out.

By design we see the Creator's handiwork in the changing
of seasons,
what beauty on display, what artistic glow.
In the changing of seasons seems to me our mood
changes as well.
In the winter frozen ice skating, cutting of wood, fireplaces
burning, popcorn cracking open, winter is here.

Ecclesiastes 3:1
To every thing there is a season, and a time to every
purpose under the heaven.

COLOR BLIND

To be color blind in a colorful world
would be a hard thing to do
to say there is no racial bias
the one that is fooled is me and you.
To me, to be color blind
is to have an unselfish point of view
until a person admits they are color blind
there is nothing no one can do.
This country has hurt long enough
you would think we'd be grown-up by now
lay our childish ways aside
and live by our constitutional vow.
That all colors are created equal
no matter if we are red, black, or brown
advance the cause of all mankind
and lay our differences down.
If you are truly color blind
sensitive to blue, violet, or an ultraviolet ray
then you are truly American
that only is OK.

*The traits of a person reveal the true character of that
individual like courage, honesty, integrity, or a bully.*

*Every day we are growing into that hewed-out person
we have become,
People are the only Bible a lot of folk ever reads.*

*2 Corinthians 3:18
But we all, with open face beholding as in a glass
the glory of the lord, are changed into the same image
from glory to glory, even as by the Spirit of the lord.*

COUNTRY CREATURES

There is the skunk and raccoon
dirty old rabbit
the weird old opossum
with its nasty old habits.
The blackbird and crow
blue jay and sparrow
field rats a runnin'
after the farmer plows with the harrow.
The bumblebee and honeybee
the dove with its woos
the dog a barkin' chasing cats.
bats swinging in the flues.
Mosquito buzzing crickets chirping
creatures on the farm
they all do their nature thing
too small to do the farmer harm.
Every day an exciting one
the farm and all its features
I wouldn't trade a single day
for the farm and its creatures.

Creatures on the farm as diverse as they were,
were a welcome sight to see.
Each one had his place, whether to annoy or help.
I believe every person, every animal, every creature
was created by the creator to serve a purpose,
the farmer knew and appreciated it.
Noah in the ark brought them in in pairs.

Genesis 7:2
Of every clean beast thou shalt take to thee by sevens,
the male and his female: and of beasts that are not clean
by two, the male and his female.

DEFENDERS OF OUR LAND

The proud, the few, the marine
fighting an enemy, elusive it seems
in a far and distant land.
You make 'em tough, we'll make 'em army tough
American soldier is ready and rough
living in foxholes and desert sand.
When you see them standing tall
or their names on the memorial wall
know they were the best America had.
Whether it was a son, daughter that gave their life
husband or devoted wife
or a new and young soldier lad.
This freedom we love and hold so dear
don't get me wrong I have some fear
of losing another soldier man
For freedoms bell to ring loud and clear
we'll need to stand and shout victory's cheer
that we all are defenders of our land.

DID YOU

Do you know where you are going
do you know where you have been
if you had to go back to the start
would you travel the same road again?
Did you learn any lessons
from mistakes you have made
of all you have accomplished
is there anything you would trade?
Have you written your best
on the pages of life's book
or do you wish there was
another path you should have took?
Lace up the bootstraps
be content where you are
what you want will never happen
if you just wish upon a star.
Put legs on your dreams
you are the one in control
be consistent in your journey
you set the goal.

DREAMIN'

Dreamin' puts you in another place
of unreal and wishful things
a place you visit often
in your own personal dreams.
It's there you lose touch with reality
and lose yourself as you knew you would
you wouldn't want to stay
in dreamland even if you could.
You enjoy every moment
being what you've always wanted to be
you stay as long as you can in dreamin'
till you return back to reality.
Dreamin' is an escape
from your present state of mind
you can visit whenever
and there unwind.
It's not wrong to go to dreamland
you know it's not real as it may seem
go there as often and do what you want
as long as you know it's only a dream.

FRESH DRINK NEW DAY

I love the smell
of a fresh morning rain
the joy of an expectant mother
in her welcomed labor pain.
The flower and grass
crops coming up
enjoying a fresh drink
from heaven's cup.
Such is the wonder
of what a new day will bring
bright sun shining
colorful birds will sing.
Each day we'll drink fresh
as it swiftly arrives
when the day is over
so will be the answers to the whys.
It's the freshness of the day
that keeps us feeling good I think
you'll only survive and wait for tomorrow
if each day you take a fresh drink.

FRIENDS

Friends are truly
a rare breed
it's someone in life
we all need.
They are someone special
you need by your side
when you are coming against
life's raging tide.
Through thick and thin
They're with you no matter what
if you are rich or poor
it doesn't matter what you got.
A friend will be a friend
wether near or far
and they take you
for who you really are.
In this day and time
be glad you still have a friend
that all is well
at day's end.

From Thirteen Stars to Fifty

From thirteen stars on old glory
to fifty that still shine
blood runs deep in her soil
part of that blood is yours and mine.
We have fought wars on different fronts
sometimes we stand alone
now we fight a different war
from the inside at home.
There is a cancerous evil
not one of honor or power
a prejudiced feeling of you done me wrong
at work still this very hour.
We must rise and admit our mistakes
lest we internally fall
time to put it to rest
here and now once and for all.
It will take all America
yellow, white, or black
forgive each our brother
then true America will be back.

Ghost of the Past

Ghost of the past
will destroy its container from within
like a parched southern crop
blown away by a hot southern wind.
Prejudice has destroyed many good men
and kept them from living free
bound by that termite of the soul
the responsibility to change lies with you and me.
Let's lay aside our differences
we all need to change for the best
pave a good road to travel
for you and I and the rest.
God created one people
he don't see the color of skin
wether you agree or not
in god's eyes we are all kin.
So let's bury the ghost of the past
never let it haunt us again
we can walk hand in hand
the way it should have always been.

GIFT OF LIFE

When I was in that dark place
I had no way to know
if I would ever be born
or would I be a no-show.
I came to be
at the moment of conception
if left up to me
I await a joyous reception.
There is a cord that binds us
until it is cut into
I remain alive
connected to you.
Please give me a chance
to live a good life
don't cut it short
with the stroke of a knife.
It's dark now
and I await to see
that person like you
that I could ever be.

GRANDPARENTING

When you had your own kids
that was joy beyond compare
keeping up with the little one
you never had a minute to spare.
Then they grew up and out
married and left home
then one day by planning
started a family of their own.
Grandkids showed up one day
I know why they are called grand
sweet as homemade pumpkin pie
we all have the grandest in the land.
Paw Paw and Neena take us there
we'll be good today
we love you all the way behind our back
every day you'd hear them say.
We would have had them first
if we would have known how grand they'd be.
money could never buy them
that's how grand they are to me.

HALF-TRUTH

In a day
when truth is hard to find
it is vague
in the face of mankind.
We want to know
what is real
help me understand
so I can feel.
No grey areas
no shades of blue
put it all on the table
let it be true.
Truth is honesty
no ifs and whys
a half-truth
is a whole lie.
Be who you are
someone that is real
nothing more powerful
than truth you can feel.

He Said She Said

He said let's go
she said oh no
he said let's dance
she said not a chance.
He said be my wife
she said not on your life
he said let's have kids
she said have you flipped your lid.
He said let's move away
she said no let's stay
he said why here
she said so I can be near.
He said next to who
she said family and you
he said we're going I am your hubby
she said so long, buddy.
He said but I love you so
she said then don't go
he said but I am your boss
she said if you leave it's your loss.

How Swift Time Flies

How swift time flies
beneath the skies
and rest beneath the
blanket of the night.
She will rise in awhile
with a brand-new smile
at the first break of light.
Let's enjoy the time
on life's page every line
bath in its beauty sublime.
When it passes from day this time
and no more sun to shine
hope that I made use of every minute that was mine.

I Don't Know

I don't know, how come,
where have you been, don't know
you been there, again and again.
Been awhile since I saw you smile,
must have been something where
you visited again and again.
I hope you do well if only you'll tell
why you're down and wear a frown,
come to me and tell, you don't have to yell.
I'll be there to listen when you cry
and maybe by and by you'll get up and try,
with less of a sigh, then I can stop asking why.
You don't get up and go, maybe a little slow
no one will know, that you got low
take your story and tell, a slight yell, that all is well.

I Saw

I saw the sadness in your eyes
the unanswerable whys
and the spent strength that had tried.
I saw the hurt that broke your heart
the thing that tore you apart
and a love gone that you couldn't restart.
I'll try to help you along
teach you a new song
let you know you are not alone.
In this struggle we call life
the pain sharp like a razor knife
thus are the demons of human strife.
I see you struggle one more time
get up and leave the past behind
knit life together like fine twine.
Now that you're back to you
and I have other things to do
your love still burns after all you've been through.

I Won't Settle for Less

I can be what I want to be
I don't have to guess
I'll rise to my expectations
I won't settle for less.
You can win or lose
you make the choice
you can go down in defeat
or rise and rejoice.
The prize is there to win
no one at the start is for sure
believe in yourself, shoot for the stars
it's yours if you will endure.
Don't listen to those that say it can't be done
if it's worth having, endure the press
go on and get what you started out for
you don't have to settle for less.
When it's all said and done
and I made it to where I purposed to be
I'll be glad I didn't give up
and accept a lesser me.

If I Had It to Do Over

If I had it to do over
there's nothing I would redo
I chose you once
again I would choose you.
If I had it to do over
I'd make better choices in life
if I had it to do over
you'd still be my wife.
If I had it to do over
I would have said I love you more
my heart was broken
when you walked out the door.
If I had it to do over
I'd say I am sorry over and over again
to have your heart completely
I'd do what I'd have to do to win.
You back to my heart
back to my home
then neither of us
would have to live alone.

If I Look Back

If I look back down the road
that I've travelled up to now
I need only focus forward
once I've put my hand to the plow.
Looking back will limit me
to the future that lies ahead
digging up bones
will only uncover the dead.
I have to rethink the day
get all my ducks in a row
and hope when the day ends
I have something to show.
If I look back to what has been
and not just repeat the words I say
I will never fulfill the Latin motto
Carpe diem—seize the day.
If you feel you have no future
and the past excites you more
on all you will ever have
you just closed the door.

In a Day

In a day when the F-word is a common slang
everyone is looking for somebody to blame
for all the bad that happened in their life
If they would step up to the plate
clear their mind and heart of hate
that would erase most all the strife.
We gotta learn how to get along
get in the same key sing the same song
in order to be free of prejudice and pride.
You gotta shake my hand
I'll greet you as my fellow man
sit in the same seat, same bus, and ride.
We brag how America is a great place to live
yet many refuse to give
different races a chance at the American dream
Stand up and say we forgive and forget
sorry for all your regret
in this day that's what's really obscene.

In God We Trust

Words paint pictures and tell stories
of who and what
pictures of what is
stories of what is or is not.
In God we trust
are not just words
you need to get out of this country
if you think in God we trust is absurd.
You can take it off our government walls
remove it from our money
if you think our trust in him is foolish
you are the one fooled, honey.
Stand up for America
tell our politicians to do the same
leave in God we trust alone
or we'll put you packin' on a go-home train.
In God we trust is a statement
of where our ability and strength lie
destroy that and its meaning
and our epitaph is, a nation dies.

In My Father's House

In my father's house are many mansions
if it were not so I would have told you
I go to prepare a place
that where I am there you can be too.
And if I go away
to that place I told you about
I will come and get you
with heavenly angels and a shout.
It has never entered
into my people's minds
the things I have laid up
are joy sublime.
It has walls of jasper
streets are paved with pure gold
gates of pearl, the lamb is the light
all these things you have been told.
Keep your garment spotless
lay aside every sin and weight
then you enter that promised land
through heaven's pearly gate.

Justice for All

Justice for all
can never be found
as long as we are searching
on the wrong ground.
Look within us
and we'll find
that the justice we want
we left behind.
In all our prejudice
we're blind and can't see
that the real problem
is with you and me.
Let's be honest and fair
truthful to all
except responsibility
no matter how the gavel falls.
We are all equal
and all to blame
justice will prevail
when we treat all the same.

LETTER ON MY INTENTIONS

When you left home
I had no way to know
where you were
or where you would go.
I prayed often
for your safe return
not knowing
that I would ever learn.
Why you left
you never said a thing
then one day
the telephone rang.
I don't know why I left
I was so confused
I want you to know
you were never used.
I left you a letter
in your Bible that day
I knew you read it often
it would tell you I just had to go away.

LIFE'S DANCE

I struggle to make it
in life's dance one more round
every time I get up
I get knocked back down.
I have no way of knowing
if the dance will be long
if I just stay in step
I'll finish the song.
The lyrics in life
are written in advance
every day you are dancing
you are taking a chance.
So grab your partner
in this dance it's you they need
embrace them closely, listen to the song
and follow their lead.
Soon the dance of life will be done
and you've made a friend
just one more verse
and the song will end.

LIFE'S TURNS

Today I watched the sun come up
the momma dog in the yard with her pup
each one had something to say
the momma dog her bark, the sun its rays.
We don't know the turns we'll take
as we journey down life's road
how fast we go
depends on our load.
We see the twists and turns
and wonder what's around the bend
whether we should change course
or this one amend.
If I don't know where I am going
then I may not know where I've been
if I don't find directions soon
I'll have to start over again.
These are the finals of life
from these lessons are learned
we must stay on course
lest we are trapped in life's turns.

LITTLE PUPPIES

Tiny little puppies
in the canine clan
I know by experience
they are the best friend to a man.
With little tiny legs
they run wabbly on their feet
so cuddly small and loving
any day they are a refreshing treat.
Each day is a new experience
as they discover who they are
careful you don't push them too hard
or on the end of your finger wear a scar.
Slowly they are adjusting
it's a challenge every day
remember in their training
they really love to play.
Reward them for their effort
let them know they fit right in
they will devote to you their honor
and stick to you through thick and thin.

LITTLE THINGS

A little mosquito
or a little gnat
can annoy you
wherever you are at.
The size is not always
what you have to worry about
and big in size
is not always stout.
A little storm
can rattle a boat
shake it to pieces
so it can't float.
What may seem to be folly
God chose little things
young little David
five smooth stones and a sling.
To defeat the giant
with a shepherd's sling
so he never would again
be fooled by the size of things.

LOST IN GOING

You can never go where you've never been
even though you try again and again.
Without exception you broke the rule
You're the only one that has been fooled.
Others have travelled down that road before
just to find out there was no door.
For them to walk through to get where they are going
all the time they are knowing.
The place where they want to go does not exist
it's fruitless for them to constantly persist.
So pack up your dreams go back to the start
realize it was only a thought from the heart.
Try searching for reality someplace you know is there
when you arrive, you'll know you were lost in going and unaware.

ME

To write is to tell
to tell is to reveal
to reveal is to know me
to know me is to be my friend
to be my friend is to walk by my side.

Mirage

We're constantly searching for truth
we need answers to the questions we ask
we don't need the facade of what might be
or the answer wearing a mask.
We don't need an optical illusion
without substance of reality
we need the truth of the matter
of how it is, not what it might be.
We travel the highway of now
and see an object of what seems true
just to find something has been displaced
in our mind all the time we knew.
That it's just wishful thinkin'
we want more out of life than we give
we should accept where we are
in this present real-time life.
At the end of the day go home
park your car in your garage
and realize when you come back to earth
all you've seen for the most part is only a mirage.

MOMMA'S JOURNEY

Momma used to sit by the window
gaze up into the skies
in her mind she had all these questions
and all her whys.
Her eyes would tell the story
you could see the hurt and pain
seemed it came often
like an everyday rain.
Momma's journey was so long
one trial after another
but she never let it stop her
from being a good mother.
Now all she can do is sit
day by day she's slipping away
most days all day
she has nothing to say.
Her life is now ending
she faces life's setting sun
her hair grey hands wrinkled
Momma's journey is done.

Morning Glories

Early morning is a refreshing time
to sit and think things over
to see the acts of nature
wet green grass and four-leaf clover.
To hear Dad sit and tell
all those old, old stories
I knew he had been many a mile
now he sits and enjoys morning glories.
To see the adorning crown
the creator placed upon this earth
is to have absolute contentment
that is man's final worth.
To admire the morning glories
the distinguished beauty untold
adorns the magnificence of the creator
as each allotted time unfolds.
Next time you gaze at the world around you
hear the voices that tell all kinds of stories
remember thy creator
he is the sum of all glories.

Daddies are a powerful figure in the lives of children.
Examples in every phase of life,
Not only are they biological figures, they are character
figures.
Daddies are superheroes, being watched by not only their
children,
but by everyone's child.
Daddy, watch your step, some child is walking in them.

1 Timothy 4:12
Let no man despise thy youth,
but be thou an example of the believers,
in word, in conversation, in charity, in spirit,
in faith, in purity.

My Name Is John Doe

They tell me
my name is John Doe
if you question me
of who I am, I don't know.
There are so many of us
our memories temporarily gone
we wander aimlessly in the day
at night we are alone.
We are trying to find ourselves
need all the help we can get
merge back into society
and be an asset.
If you see a John Doe
lend them a hand
help them to find
the woman or man.
They used to be
before they lost it all
and be who they were
before the fall.

Never Put Off

Don't put off for tomorrow
what you can do today
take the necessary steps
you'll find a way.
It's never really that hard
to do what you want to do
just make sure
that you follow through.
To put off is to say no
to the success of the now
when day wears on and is done
you'll only wander how.
You let it slip by
when you could have done more
to that time and moment
you have closed the door.
Realize all you'll ever have
is what you get by the way
never put off for tomorrow
what you can do today.

NINE ELEVEN

When we woke up
on that sunny day
everyone was starting out
going their separate way.
The enemy suddenly struck
to achieve their goal
America was wounded
deep in her soul.
We wept in pain
at what we had lost
no one could tally
up the awful cost.
We buried our dead
and rose to say
we will not stand for
anyone doing us that way.
We'll fight to the end
till our work is done
and we'll never forget
what the enemy done on nine one one.

No Matter What

I love you no matter what
you say or do to me
my love is not just on the surface
it's deep where you can't see.
When we started this relationship
I told you I love you dear
nothing means more to me
than having you near.
Trust me when I tell you
I meant my love for life
that's why tonight with this ring
I ask you to be my wife.
Your love has filled my emptiness
and made me feel grand
just to know you chose me
to always be your man.
The cord we share is strong
I guess what I am trying to say
is, darling, I hope toward me
you feel the same way.

No More

I never thought about this much
till one day I found
that I should have said I love you daily
'cause you want always be around.
God reached down and took you
only he knew the pain we bore
it was that day it came to me so vividly
she is with us no more.
No more hugs and kisses
no more phone calls too
God said come to me
now no more you.
No more time to think about
the mistakes I made in life
no more time to take it back
and now no more wife.
Please don't let time pass you by
soon enough you'll see
that brother, sister, Mom, Dad, and children
they one day no more will be.

No Name

I am a no-name
I travel the road of life
I am someone's daughter
or maybe someone's wife.
When you see me on the road
stop and ask me who I am
I may be a Sallie Ann
or maybe a Sam.
Somehow I've lost my way
please help me find myself
in the refuse of life
to gather up what's left.
To walk in circles daily
try to find the who
to put a name on me
I'll need help from you.
Call them what you may
no one is to blame
they are the victim of the times
just be glad you got a name.

OH, MOON, OH, MOON

Oh, moon, oh, moon
tell me please
give me the answer
while I'm on my knees.
I need help
I can't do it, I've tried
move for me
like you move the sea's tide.
You roll the sea in
and roll it out
move the giant waves
draw up the waterspouts.
So, moon, oh, moon
today you are new
if I could
I'd jump over you.
Oh, moon, on moon
guide me to my love
help me to find her
oh, light from above.

OUR JOURNEY

Our journey started
when you took me by the hand
I devote myself to you, darling
you are my man.
It has been a long one
a lot of twist and turns along the way
we managed to hold it together
I love you, to each other we would say.
Time and trials have tested our resolve
but we loved each other more
no matter how shaky things got
we both remained sure.
That our love is deeper than the trials
wider than the sea
because I was meant for you
and you were meant for me.
We'll keep sharing our love together
as we are growing old
may this marriage and our love
never, never grow cold.

POWER TO BECOME

In each one of us
is the power to choose
by making our choices
we either win or lose.
In the beginning
the creator gave us some
gifts and talents
the power to become.
If we don't reach forward
we can never know
if we could have it
could it ever be so.
The power to become
is leaving where we are
developing into that image of God
without leaving a scar.
We should never look back
to where we are from
I am what I am
glad of what I have become.

PREJUDICE

Prejudice is a bitter evil
that infects every generation
we need to leave the ghosts behind
and be an unbiased nation.
Come out of these you-owe-me feelings
black or white it's wrong
let's get on and heal our wounds
the time has been too long.
America is a great country
we've won wars abroad and at home
if you listen on a quiet day
sadly you can hear prejudice moan.
Many refuse to say I am wrong
they'd rather live with the prejudice than try
to help this country heal itself
they had rather die.
Let's girt up the loins of our mind
all colors not just one
and be a nation under God
that has overcome.

The person that discriminates in this season of life,
is very much out of step, this is not the fifties or sixties.
Every man every woman every race every color are
God's creation, we all are equal in the creator's eyes.

Romans 2:11
For there is no respect of persons with God.

James 2:9
But if ye have respect of persons, ye commit sin,
and are convinced of the law as transgressors.

RED, WHITE, AND BLUE

Our men and women
come from all around
rural American cities too
and maybe your town.
A stranger from afar
maybe someone you knew
they dawn America's colors
the red, white, and blue.
Our heroes from the past
to them we humbly bow
let's not forget their sacrifice
or those brave heroes now.
They serve our country well
they that wear the uniform
they are our heroes
they are not of the norm.
The next time you see a soldier
raise your hand and salute
they are our heroes from the past and now
they are the absolute.

Ribbons from Your Hair

Ribbons from your hair
baby clothes you wear
you were an angel sent from above.
You lit up our home
so we wouldn't be alone
shared with us all your love.
Toddler clothes and toys
sad times and joys
you were our promised child
Crawling on the floor
first steps and more
the beauty in your little smile.
We watch you growing up
shedding diapers and sippy cups
no more dolls and little curly trains.
Growing out of clothes
that woman starts to show
you are just dealing with growing pains.

SLEIGHT OF THE HAND

A sleight of the hand
can fool a man
on the ground a fooled man will land.
If you have been deceived
you must have believed
in the wicked web you weaved
If I try to get free
I soon will see
the web I weaved caught me.
So rise from despair
get a breath of fresh air
you've been released from the snare.
Out of the deceiver's hand you left
where you had sit like a whatnot on a shelf
you only had fooled yourself.

STATUS QUO

Status quo
is staying where you are
never going forward
to see how far.
It is to where you're going
but you'll never know
if you stand still
and accept status quo.
Status quo
is having no desire
accepting no furtherance
so there you retire.
If you're gonna have anything
you gotta step up
quit sipping from the saucer
start drinking from the cup.
Step up to the plate
hit the ball that's thrown
for the grand slam
you'll always be known.

STEPS OF A HOMELESS MAN

When things had got so bad
failure was an everyday drink
he daily fought to stay afloat
he knew he was about to sink.
He wrote down on that legal pad
how he planned to fix it all
instead a fix fixed him that day
he was alone when he took the fall.
He grabbed a brown paper bag
a few wrinkled clothes inside
he walks away looking back
a homeless man with broken pride.
He struggled to pick up his broken man
get his life and family back
up and on with his life
away from a homeless man's tracks.
In your effort to avoid responsibility
you sunk deeper in the muck and mire
if you don't take lessons from mistakes you've made.
you are jumping out of the frying pan into the fire.

The Altar

The altar is a place of commitment
where we as individuals tell all
emptying our souls young and old
kneeling down, we stand tall.
It is a place of sacrifice
where we release what's held us back
lay down the old, pick up the new
that in us, there is no lack.
The altar is where death occurred
there the blood would spill
laying aside the weights and sin
so that one could do God's will.
At the altar it was a dreadful place
will against will would fight
blow after blow to tear away
that when over, one could see the light.
Don't think that the altar is against you
it has big ears when you come to pray
the God of the altar's purpose
is all is well at the end of the day.

The Day Before

The day before I met you
I was empty and lonely inside
I couldn't make myself happy
no matter how I tried.
The day before we married
I was the happiest man on earth
now that we are married
we know each other's worth.
The day before we had our first child
I couldn't hardly wait
I walked the floor twiddling my thumbs
hoping you wouldn't be late.
The day before she married
I thought at home she would always stay
but a young prince stole you
and moved you away.
The day before we had our first grandchild
to be happier I couldn't see how
then when he was born
all I could say was wow.

THE EXTRAVAGANCE OF GOD

You see the finger of God
everywhere you travel
it seems to say
it's God's way to unravel.
The mysteries of the creator
in every place you'll find
his extravagance glowing
on the face of mankind.
From the tiniest gnat
that gets in your face
the flower in full color
in the evening bows in grace.
Oceans and seas birds and bees
can't explain it don't try
the flowers and trees all come to life
at the end of its season it dies.
So is the mystery
of God's wonderful plan
only true beauty
is in the creator's hand.

THE STORM

The storm is pounding
in an uncontrolled surrounding
we're near drowning.
We try rowing to the shore
our strength is no more
the wrath of the sea we bore.
We now feel the end
the ship about to bend
SOS we send.
We wait for a light
in the frightened night
nothing in sight.
In the distance now I see
a light staring at me
I long to be free.
I am losing my fear
I have nothing but cheer
the lighthouse is near.

THE UNKNOWN

The unknown haunts us
like a ghost in the night
we search to know
and we still have no light.
The unknown is elusive
and no matter how smart we get
when the search is all done
all we have is regret.
We searched over here
and searched over their
at the close of the day
we're still unaware.
That it cannot be found
no matter how hard you try
it will still be unknown
in the sweet by and by.
We should be content
in whatever state we're in
quit the search and be happy
and you win.

THESE COLORS DON'T RUN

These colors don't run
the red, white, and blue
it that's what you are thinkin'
then shame on you.
We don't like to shed blood
if we do that's okay
we'll fight you tooth and nail
so old glory can still wave.
America has paid a high price
loss of our daughters and sons
we want our enemies to know
these colors just won't run.
We are a people of pride
just thankful to be free
from border to border over this land
and sea to shining sea.
The next time you see these colors
stand right up and salute
know that our resolve is firm
and our purpose absolute.

TRUST

Love is what holds
a relationship together
when joined by two
any storm you can weather.
Love is like a house
made into a home
in order for it to stand
it must have a strong foundation to build on.
The foundation of that home
is an absolute must
my experience in life
I found that foundation to be trust.
Trust is more
than a five-letter word
it's the strongest bond between two
to some it may seem absurd.
Try it you'll like it
it will keep two people in love strong
will hold you together
when things in life go wrong.

TWIST OF THE WIND

A twist of the wind
is a change of mind
of a path once taken
but now left behind.
Take the path
that fate leads you down
it comes from a gut feeling
not from a certain sound.
The wind will keep blowing
bringing life's different smells
what's in the bucket
came up from the well.
No one knows
what tomorrow may hold
whether it's life's silver lining
or a fool's gold.
Continue your journey
in all that you do
remember while making choices
choices are making you.

Unknown

Enquiring minds
want to know
is it false
or is it so.
We want the news
before it comes out
tell me I gotta know
I don't want to do without.
To not know
what's around the bend
keeps us wandering
if and when.
To know what's on tomorrow
could hurt me so
I think I'll refuse
to want to know.
I'll just take life
one day at a time
quit wandering about the unknown
and relish what's mine.

WE ARE ALL ONE

In this span we call life
each day is new
the success of our future
depends on me and you.
God didn't create
yellow, brown, black, or white
he made us all one
that we could walk in the same light.
Quit cutting down your fellow man
slappin' him in the face
saying he don't belong
criticizing his race.
There's no big Is and little yous
in this race we're all to run
so it doesn't matter how you and I feel
in God's eyes we are all one.

WE DON'T KNOW TOMORROW

We don't know tomorrow
what life will bring
a sad note or two
or a new song to sing.
One thing we know for sure
when we get there we'll be here
close to where we want to be
if not there, at least we'll be near.
We have to take every advantage
of the opportunities we get
after all life
is simply a bet.
Not knowing the future
we must make every step sure
knowing that alone will give us
the will to endure.
Since we are limited in our insight
and can only go so far
we will live with uncertainty
because we don't know what's on tomorrow.

WE TAKE THIS AND THAT

We take this we take that
trying to get healthy
watch this video and that video
to learn how to get wealthy.
We take pills to lose weight
pills to help our mind
pills to speed up
pills to unwind.
All kinds of vitamins
to build up our immune system
everything you can think of
to get us back in tune.
Lord knows what's next
so be careful what you take
it may help you so far along
you want be able to awake.
Ask someone to help you
if you are not able
oh yes
be sure to read the label.

WE THE PEOPLE

We the people
are of a peculiar kind
all can walk by our side
we don't mind.
But when you start
to destroy our liberties
and we let them go unchallenged
then we are no longer free.
We founded this great country
on principles of in God we trust
for freedom to still reign
belief in those principles is still a must.
We the people
is the strength of this nation
for we the people to go on and through
we all have an obligation.
For moral fibers
in our country they once have been
let's get 'em back remain united
and we the people win.

WHERE TWO WAYS MEET

Each day that we live we have choices to make, should we do this
or should we wait? Should I go there or go over yonder
or just mark time sit here and wander. Each day I travel
I become more discreet then I reach that place where two ways
meet.
Where two ways meet is a place of choice, will I let it confuse me
or will I rejoice. I must make the ultimate decision
even if I fail at least I tried.

Wonders of Creation

The breathless sky wonders and whys
of how all this came about
when you see the beauty of earth and its worth
in your mind there is no doubt.
That we are not a product of evolution
we didn't just happen to be
when you see the beauty of humanity unfold
it's plain for all to see.
That in the mystic beyond where the answer lies
where there is a creator of all
with every breath and every word
he has painted the answer on life's wall.
Let's figure it out and remove the doubt
as we skip over this land of sod and trod
that in all, good or bad
there is the image of God.
In every way a trace of DNA
let's me know we are part of wonders of creation
in the height of it all we beckoned to the call
in the wonders of creation humanity is the summation.

Words I Never Said

Words are powerful tools
they can build up or tear down
if left unsaid
they are thoughts with no sound.
If you ever wanted to say a word
for some reason it was never said
all you'll have to live with
is a lifelong of dread.
That you never spoke your heart
and said it for all to hear
words never spoken
will never draw you near.
To the friend that is the best
or a love that is real
what you never said
they can never feel.
Say your words with feeling
and you will never dread
of having to live with
what you never said.

YOU AND I

You and I sit and wonder why
things don't get better by and by
is everything just pie in the sky.
Can I do something to make a change
to my ability rearrange
so that what we see won't be strange.
I'll give my two cents to help along
try not to embrace the inquisitive throng
and cushion the body that is on loan.
From the creator far above
expressing to all his tender love
help me not to get behind and shove.
You from your position in line
that you attained when you had a good mind
you and I must follow the line this time.
I'll do what I can, really try
maybe now and then a sigh
the consummation of all, is in you and I.

MY CONTRIBUTION TO TODAY

Dedication to GOD and Country

I realize as I awoke today,
from the sleep GOD gave to me.
how delicate, sweet, and precious
life could be, if I let it Be.

So today I make my contribution
of what GOD gave from the start
Let it be, it must be,
straight from the heart.

I will be too thee and me
what I must be today
unfolding, unwinding
It won't happen, can't be, so the critics say.

But you'll see me I'll be there
as I contribute my handful of worth
no one can stop me, I can't be stopped
my gift to GOD's beautiful earth.

A Price to Pay

I saw the land how big it was
and all the fruit thereof
to get that fruit in my hand
would be my firm resolve.
I realize there would be
a price I'd have to pay
if I am going to be rich in fruit
today must be the day.
For all that I would pay
would be just a mite you see
to reach all my goals in life
is left entirely up to me.
The giants they do dwell in the land
their size I cannot tell
I am convinced they'll spook and run
at one apostolic holy ghost yell.
If the enemy has taken your spoil away
left you to weep and cry
rise and declare the giant is just a speck
get back the fruit money can't buy.

ADOPTION

Don't know my mommie and daddy
they gave me away before my birth
and when I make my entrance
I'll have no earthly worth.
Lying in the baby ward
though I could hardly see
they're against the window
I saw four eyes staring down at me.
Looks of joy and hope
filled the wrinkles in her and him
they signed the papers and took me home
like me, they needed someone to love them.
I know my tiny turned-up toes
cute little dimples and rosy nose
filled your heart with lots of joy
you didn't care if I was a girl or boy.
Now I am getting older I can plainly see
that you had the heart of a mom and dad
you had a choice, and you chose me.

AMERICA FREE

This country was founded on principles
by Christians at Plymouth Rock
if you're thinking of changing that
you better find another port to dock.
'Cause this ship is firmly anchored
to beliefs you don't understand
and we have a God-given right
to defend America our land.
Her soil is rich in red blood
our freedom secure and true
and any day from Monday to Sunday
America can outdo you.
Some have tried to sneak right in
and break her will to stand
same old song again and again
it's unity they don't understand.
All may not be perfect
we're working on that as well
I can assure you when sun sets today
our freedom is still not for sale.

America Is Still Great

From the battlefields of Tennessee
to the western plains and town
we've made it to this freedom place
'cause someone stood their ground.
All love the colors of ole glory
and its stripes we gladly bear
if you're thinking of hurting us
for your sake don't even dare
We are diverse in our thinking
our opinions we share with all
if you think that makes us weak
just try us and you will fall.
We fought down segregation
said it won't be anymore
laid our differences down for good
that we might live on the same shore.
God bless America
it's still a great place to be
and we'll defend her still today
from sea to shining sea.

BIG CITY HUMBLE COUNTRY

I went into the big city
from the country where I grew up
folks were hustling and bustling
with backpack computer and full coffee cup
Off to work they were going
hail a taxi or big city bus
gotta punch in at eight or nine
so I gotta go in a rush.
The big city pressure is rising
more folks now than before
the country don't have all that
one hardly ever knocks at the door.
In the country we're all laid-back
we choose the pace we'll go
whether to go in the fast lane
or hold it down and go slow.
City folks live to work
country folks work to live
you'll hold life together
if you learn of yourself to give.

CHANGING SEASONS

Crystal snowflakes fall so bright
cover the cold ground in the night
so pure and clean it feels in hand
part of the mystery of heaven grand.
Then the cold leaves the air
and ushers in the spring so fair
rain falls the wind blows
everyone waits for spring to go.
The leaves turn and soon rot
summer arrives always hot
the crops come on and yield its grain
it is an amazing thing.
Now summers gone and heat as well
fall arrives no one can tell
how all the seasons come and go
only the creator has wisdom to know.
So enjoy all the season change
and never want to rearrange
what the creator did with his hand
all across this great land.

CONSTITUTION PEOPLE

The founding fathers wrote our constitution
we the people pledge our all
thirteen men dedicated
that this new union would not fall.
These articles were written
with the will of the people at heart
and we should remain with them
like we did at the start.
They bore out a government
with principles and rights
and declared they would defend them
even if they had to fight.
Millions of lives have paid the price
honor don't come cheap
stand at our burial sites
hear the widows weep.
All men are created equal
that stands from then till now
from Connecticut to Virginia
with unity we'll make it somehow.

CONTRARY WIND

When I went to sleep last night
all seemed so very well
Then the day dawned upon me
don't know if I can tell.
How swift the wind was blowing
though I could hardly see
what was really happening
and how it was changing me.
In a moment life was changing
contrary wind so real and strong
two steps forward two back
it all seemed so very wrong.
Can't explain the sudden decline
and how the wind came rushing through
all now seems so uncertain
I don't know what to do
So I'll just steady the course
steer as hard as I can
and pray when the wind dies down
I'll be more of a man.

COUNTRY LIVING

We got up early in the mornin'
built a fire to heat the place
set the food on the table
while Momma said the grace.
Day would go on and wind down
we'd gather the kindlin' to build a fire
keep the pot belly stove hot
until we would retire.
Lay down on an old pallet
by the old rusty screen door
just tryin' to get comfortable
on that old hardwood floor.
There were no lights to turn out
just a lamp we'd turn down
we slept like a baby
till we heard the rooster sound.

DAY HAPPENINGS

The sun that sets
and brings the night
night disappears
brings the day bright.
The day comes on
with its answers unfound
we search to find them
when no one's around.
The hot sun unleashed
upon our tender skin
wished for the shade
and a breath of wind.
Day happenings are a mystery
no one knows
how she comes in
or how swift she goes.
We pray for the night
and watch it settle in
day will soon come
the same all over again.

DEVOTED SOLDIER

He came out of the battlefield
wounded but alive
said fix me up I'm going again
if I have to walk or drive.
I gotta get my wounds all healed
thanks for your love and care
I am a devoted soldier
my buddies need me there.
We're fighting for a reason
our freedom is not free
when I'm asked to guard our wall
it's there you'll find me.
I'm given to the cause at hand
won't let the critics get me down
I'd rather win our freedom there
than to fight here on our ground.
I lift up high old glory
its stars and stripes the way
tear fills my eyes, I'm grateful
for this good old USA.

DOWN AND OUT

When I am down and out
I try to shout but can't get out

Of this slump I am in
so I begin to grope again

To be set free and be to thee
what you desire of me.

Help me help me pull me along
You can do it, you are the strong.

Been down long enough
Tired of sippin' from down's cup.

I've now broke out from being down
from here on OUT it's the sky not the ground

DOWN HOME LIVING

Let me tell you how it used to be
when I was growing up
Momma cooked in an old coal stove
Daddy drank coffee from an old tin cup.
We gathered round the table
so Momma could say grace
we all knew where to sit
each one had his place.
Momma's chicken beat Colonel Sanders
her apple pie beat Martha Whites
you knew it could win a fair contest
when you took that very first bite.
Down home living
from the country point of view
hard country working
there was no easy thing to do.
Every body pitched right in
to get all the work done
then we'd go to the swimming hole
have the country kind of fun.

EARLY MORNING COUNTRY

Early in the morning
sippin' coffee hot and strong
chirping birds and glittering dew
been sittin' here don't know how long.
I tried not to rush things
just wanted to be able
to enjoy the quiet in early morning
and wait for breakfast on the table.
So I sit and watch the sun rise
in the east far away
introducing to us all
another bright and sunny day.
Looking at the eastern sun
I saw dancing in the silhouette
all kinds of flying morning creatures
glitter of dew that made the ground wet.
Early morning country time
I waited for it every day
sippin' coffee reading the paper
the morning always had something to say.

Elusive Me

I am here
because I am not there
and if you've searched
for me everywhere.
Look in your mind
see if you can find
where I am
and after that.
If you still can't find me
look in your dreams
and if I am not there
by now it seems.
It's elusive me
you can't find me at all
I am inconspicuous
as a fly on the wall.
The reason you can't find me
I love being alone
I'll remain elusive
I don't want to be known.

ENDURING LOVE

Enduring love is a wonderful thing
its limits you cannot measure
the glitter and glow so perfectly beautiful
it truly is a treasure.
It knows no boundaries
like a tree it stands tall
sweet as a fresh morning flower
placed on life's wall.
Like a giant bridge
it connects two sides
brings them together
even against the tide.
It's devoted and true
desire remains strong
like a passionate love story
written in a song.
It never quits
goes on without end
it's stronger now
than when it began.

Finding My Place

Momma always told me
there is a reason for being here
and every step and choice you make
each day draws you near.
Make all the right decisions
think about them very well
and those following your footsteps
can stand right up and tell.
that you got knocked down a time or two
and got back up again
struggling each day to make it
it's better now than then.
It's not in me to give up
throw in the towel and say I am done
or to accept a lesser me
in this race I've run.
I've reached that place
Momma told me I would find
I accept where I am
and leave the other life behind.

FORGOTTEN HEROES

We sometimes forget our heroes
from days gone by
never seem to get an answer
or know the reason why.
They fell on the battlefield
on some far and distant shore
the widows stood and wept in tears
when news came to their door.
From the island of Okinawa
to the shores of Normandy
not a life fell in vain
for that we are free.
In the rice patties of Vietnam
the horror still relived
the Veterans' nerves and mind gone
they have nothing left to give.
Let's remember the sacrifice
the high price they had to pay
so you and I could live free
in this great country USA.

HOMELESS

Life dealt him a bad hand
one he can't play
so he puts all in a bag
and is on his way.
He don't know where he's going
or how to get there
frustrated with his life
he feels no one cares.
He stands on the corner
with sign in his hand
I'll work please help
I am a hungry man.
Why is it in this country
the land of the free
we pass them right up
and say they're nothing to me.
Let's gather up our soul
help the homeless on the street
and maybe the next time
it won't be you that you meet.

How It Used to Be

Daddy plowed the cotton fields
Momma sang a song
days were not eight hours
they were hot and long.
Daddy drank black coffee
Momma drank it too
everybody worked real hard
we all knew what to do.
The seasons would come and go
all would lay up in store
we could always go to our neighbor
if we ever needed more.
I sit here now aging
seems I can hardly see
now you get things on demand
that's not the way it used to be.
So we can only adjust ourselves
and try to fit right in
hold on to our precious memories
And wish it could be like it was back then.

How Life Was in Arkansas

Daddy planted the cotton field
the roes sometimes had a bend
said you could get more on them
if there was a curve every now and then.
Seedtime would turn to harvesttime
no one got much rest
the gins ran 24/7
everyone doing their best.
To get all the grain in
prepare for school in the fall
wait for winter snowflakes
and be happy one and all.
The ground got so hard
from the winter cold that came
spring rolled in we livened up
then went out the same.
That's the way it came year after year
it least that's the way I saw
life on a cotton farm
in northeast Arkansas.

IT'S A SAD DAY

It's a sad, sad day
in this our land
when there are those among us
that refuse to let truth stand.
They fight the court system
try to get 'em to change the plan
say they are red-blooded Americans
but refuse to shake your hand.
This country is made up of people
from every race and from all walks of life
each has their opinion
so let's sit down and talk.
Agree that we are diverse
respect each of your fellow man
and when you're challenged to stand up
he'll be there to take your hand.
I'll respect you and you respect me
our opinions as we walk along
let's agree and disagree
and sing America, America the song.

It's Our Land

It's our land America
home of the brave and free
tomorrow we'll defend her
on land and on sea.
We say yes to go abroad
for freedom's victory call
the names that have sacrificed
are in Washington on a wall.
It's America our land
there is a price we have to pay
so we go hand in hand together
and not have to change our ways.
The soldiers of this democracy
are rare proven and true
they say we shouldn't be fighting among us
it doesn't matter which party you belong to.
Let's get our heads out of the sand
hold our brothers hand in hand
then we can successfully defend her
America it's our land.

LEND A HELPING HAND

We need to be more sensitive
lend them a helping hand
let our elderly folks know
the grey hair they have is grand.
The hitchhiker on the highway
that's been passed up by all
fix a flat on the road
answer emergency call.
Mow a yard for the handicap
push a grocery cart for an elderly man
give a dollar to the homeless
lend a helping hand.
We've neglected to see their need
so we give them a chair or cane
marked them off as just old folk
dealing with their pain.
Thank God for the elderly
they help make us what we are
we should do for all of them
the end is not far.

LIFE'S CHOIR

As I travel all around
from far and near I hear the sound
like beating drums far away
every voice has something to say.
The tenor voice and bass so low
Distinguishes for all that want to know
what says the voice what does it mean
you can only hear it can't be seen.
I hear politics with words they weave
most don't know what they believe
with sounding attacks against fellow man
they mute the voice that was so grand.
The voice of pain sounds, tones of grief
while voices of healing bring relief
sun sounds hot and rain so fresh
nurtures the soul and cheers the flesh.
Life's choir sings with all its strain
help comfort you with less pain
So make your voice clear and strong
You now are singing life's final song.

LIFE'S JOURNEY

I lost my way the other day
then I heard somebody say
you can travel this way if you may
The road was rough as I travelled along
I prayed I wouldn't take the wrong
I kept going forward with less of a moan
A cloud by day fire by night
where I was going was not in sight
I will keep travelling till I see the light
I want to give up, I want to give in
been heading this way since way back when
I am closer now than back then.
If time don't catch me and slow me down
I'll keep on going till I am in the ground.
When there is silence no more sound.
This is my purpose for being here
step by step he draws me near
now in the distance angels cheer.

LIFE'S PROCESS

A constant dripping of sorrow
little needles that prick the heart
life's continuous drops of water
wears us away part by part.
We stagger to make it along
in the darkness we fail to see
that maybe something greater is calling
to bring us to perfection you and me.
I keep struggling to see the light
and make it another mile
slowly by determination
I grow into manhood from a child.
I realize life's ups and downs
are meant to mold us near
to the image of our creator
not in eyes of our peer.
I will not bow again at all
nor yield to pressure from below
I've reached the place I was meant to be
though the process was long and slow.

LOVE

Love is more than butterflies
or funny feelings down deep
it's an overwhelming sensation
that robs you of your sleep.
It's more than little kisses
or sitting holding hands
more than building sand castles
with your sweet love in the sand.
More than writing love notes
or blowing kisses in the wind
or making sneaky phone calls
trying to hide it from next of kin.
It's two people that come together
fall in love along the way
till death do us part
to eternity you'll hear them say.

MAKING AND MOLDING

A little thread stitch by stitch
We are slowly sewn together
It will happen regardless of our resistance
No matter the kind of weather.
Help along your fellow man
Pick him up when he falls
And maybe when you are down and out
He'll gladly answer the call.
It's not about what you get
It's what you give that counts
Each and every good you do
Will be added to your account
To pick you up and get you going
Rescue you from your sad demise
It was not meant to exploit your will
But rather make you wise.
Then one day you can cash it in
You can get and not give
Because of your contribution
You made America a better place to live.

MOMMA TRIED

Momma used to pray out loud
and sing the songs of Zion
no matter how down she got
She never did stop tryin'.
She worked in the cotton field
And cooked three meals a day
Wore her hands to the bone
To make a better way.
Momma seemed to be content
She knew GOD was on her side
She would go forward then fall back
No matter how she tried.
She would walk for miles to go to church
and bring the kids along
Shout around the pot belly stove
And sing "Amazing Grace" the song.
Momma's gone no one to pray
Life's tasks we must not shun
We need to walk the walk, talk the talk
Until all she started is done

MOMMA WAS AN ANGEL

I used to hear Momma tell the story
how times were hard but never got her down
food on the table tomorrow
today we get it from the ground
Momma was an angel among us
she dressed our wounds and let us play again
her steps were steady God was first
that's the way it was way back then.
Momma couldn't give us what she wanted
to buy us clothes when she would go to town
her heart was broke, but love showed through
all we had to wear was hand-me-downs.
Through the years and lots of disappointment
Momma lost her hold on life she knew
frail and weak our angel was leaving
yet she remained faithful and true.
God reached down and took our angel
moved her to a far and distant land
though your presence can't be seen from earth's view
I know you're in that place called heaven grand.

POETRY FOR MOMMA

From the time I can remember
Don't know if it was January or December
Of your love so warm and true
Folks didn't know what they were missing if they didn't know you.
Her firmness great, when you kids go out don't be late.
Like a mother hen she watched over us way back then.
She defeated adversity oftentimes weak
She always made sense when she would speak.
You dared not ignore the things she said
Or else you would be bent over the bed
To taste her correction in a stinging kind of touch.
Child, it's because I love you, Momma don't love me so much.
Her unselfish ways and smile lit the sky
All was affected even the passerby.

POVERTY OH POVERTY

I used to know a little boy
on the farm where I was raised
he always seemed so happy
because of that I was amazed.
His shoes and clothes were hand-me-downs
he was happy no matter what
and boy you'd sure know
if new clothes he ever got.
I saw him on the road one day
in the summertime back then
holes in his shoes patch on his pants
he hadn't got a hand-me-down again.
Just the same he was happy
you could see it in his walk
you'd never have a doubt
if you ever heard him talk.
Being poor never bothered him
you could tell it when you'd see
he wasn't a stranger no one knew
that poor boy was me.

Raising Children a Journey

Man and woman marries
they both become one
as they make life's journey
their work is never done.
The wife becomes a momma
new life in the home
all the things she went through
up to now are gone.
Tending to this gift from God
makes Momma's work a joy
she really didn't care
if it was a girl or boy.
Momma's job intensifies
the child is growing up
trash the diapers and little wippies
and throw away the sippy cup.
Dad and Mom has worked real hard
though the journey sometimes wild
their baby is all grown up now
it is no longer a child.

SPECIAL FRIENDS

We started this journey
when you shook my hand
together we both took a stand.
To show each other's
deserved respect
and the needs of each other never neglect.
'Cause friendship is sharing a dream or two
about what each other might do
at the same time to each be true.
It's not about having my way
and never listen to what you gotta say
your opinion concerns me today.
In our shared friendship I felt I must
have someone special I could trust.
You have proven to me over again
that you truly are my special friend
and as of this moment we have nothing to mend.
I hope in our journeys you plainly see
that I was the same friend you were to me.

STEPS OF LIFE

We're really uncertain
how things will be
each step we take
we're more able to see.
Life comes into view
the process begins
only God in heaven
knows how long it's been.
Since we took the first step
on the direction we'll take
we get closer each day
as choices we make.
Steps of life
must be careful each time
so we don't step wrong
and get off the line.
Head down some road
where we've never been
forget all the steps we've taken
and have to start over again.

THE SETTING SUN

As I sit here reminiscing
over my life and the past
I realize I must hurry
don't know how much longer I will last.
How swift life is
like a vapor it's gone
leaving you with aches
and a waning moan.
My hands started hurting
aches and pain in my back
I used to know everything that happened
but now I am losing track.
Now I am in retirement
got trouble with my heart
it's a lot more foggy now
that it was at the start.
I hope I don't end up in a nursing home
that's a place I don't wanna be
the sun is setting on my life
it's hazier than it used to be.

TIME

I know there is a season
and a time for everything
Under this great heaven
So says the words of a king.
We see the crops planted in the fields
then comes the sun and rain
And one day not far down the road
We harvest in the grain.
Then because of an evil soul
Some rob, cheat, and kill
Then knowledge comes doctors learn
In time they began to heal.
Some will gather up a stone
Toss it in his fellow man's face
While others will be the gift of GOD
Pull man to his bosom and embrace
Now in a time of God knows what
it seems we barely stood the test
if we are to make it work
All must do his best.

TRUSTED FRIEND

The trusted hand of a dear friend
speaks volumes to the soul of a man
knowing we weathered a lot of storms
makes our friendship grand.
It's not based on always saying yes
or of our friendship one might guess
it's about a knot one can't see
a bond between two, you and me.
I drew so much strength
from the times we had spent
I tried to relent
when you up and went.
To follow your dreams
to me now seems
we have nothing to mend
you're my trusted friend.
Our cord is still strong
doesn't matter how long
we're apart
I am glad we made the start.

Unfolding Mysteries

Life's unfolding mysteries
we see them every day
don't know how to explain it
to define, no words to say
One thing we know for certain
we go with its changing or get left behind
yield ourselves to the changer
and be happy we still got a mind.
Now take the ole bumblebee
scientists say cannot fly
yet he lifts up his wings
soars against impossibilities deep into the sky.
The rose unfolds its petals
expose its beauty on life's wall
we wander in amazement
to their purpose at all.
The tadpole don't stay a tadpole
it yields to a higher stage
then moves on to another level
that's written on another page.

WESTERN SUNSET

I watched the sun set in the west
and wondered what the night would bring
shooting stars glowing moon
and the owl in his own way sings.
The darkness has a lonely touch
its voices has things to say
Milky Way and the Big Dipper
streetlights that reminds you of the day.
You yawn for sleep
for your weary eyes
the blanket of stars
that fills the skies.
They say to you
it's time to turn in
sweet dreams and night thoughts
wait for the new day to begin.
Then the sun comes up
and dawns upon you
excited and rested
glad the night is through.

YESTERDAY AND TOMORROW

As we travel through life
over land and sea
we steady are grasping
for two places we cannot be.
You can't get there from where you are
even if you wished
upon a falling star.
If you focus on yesterday's failures
or tomorrow's might be's
you lose the gift of now
and will never be free.
Remember you can't have
what you never had
quit chasing elusive rainbows
in the present be glad.
If you are in pursuit of happiness
leave yesterday and tomorrow alone
embrace what you have where you are
at least two of your troubles will be gone.

WHEN I AWOKE

When I woke this morning
I felt so free
The fingers of freedom touching me.

Seemed so much beauty
Surrounded me so
I was off to greet the world
With a sigh and a glow.

Happy smiling faces
Lit the sidewalk so bright
I was so happy
Tried to wish away the night

But in the rush of a moment
Events darkened the sun
America was wounded
On nine one one.

We weep through the pain
Pick up the pieces and go on
We'll never forget the heroes
Whose voices still echo on the phone.

A Soldier's Point of View

The first time he wrote home
he was an excited soldier man
we're here doing a lot of good, Momma
in this far and distant land.

The next time he wrote home
he had a different point of view
Momma, if we don't fight here
they'll come there and hurt you.

I am defending our great country
I don't fully understand
why folks just can't get along
and love their homeland.

Freedom is never free
it's red to every grave
the sacrifice we made is worth it
so old glory can still wave.

The last time he wrote home
his paper was stained with tears
you could tell he was broken
and that his time was drawing near.

Mom waited for a letter today
instead the military come
the president is sorry
for the loss of your son.

Sad Day

It was a sad day in America
when she prostituted her soul
you could tell her mind-set
when they went to the polls.

She has murdered the unknown millions
let's remove in God we trust
oh yea, you gotta be law biding
obey the law you must.

Some try to say it's not Merry Xmas
because they are not merry at all
America, better wake up soon
the handwriting is on the wall.

It's a peace-loving country
or at least that's the way it should be known
the courts bind the hands of policemen
and let the criminal roam.

Some say they want a free America
but when it's time to defend they run
because they don't want to sacrifice
a daughter or son.

It's a tragedy to lose a daughter or son
to any conflict or war
to see their blood spilt
in a land off so far.

America is built on a set of rules and principles
guarded by the free and brave
if they are not kept in sacred trust
then ole glory will no longer wave.

OLD FOLK

The seasons of time
it comes and goes
leaving us with grey hair
white as winter snow.

A process of life
we all go through
we couldn't change a thing
even if we knew.

How it all works
or when the end will be
slurring of speech
or eyes that faintly see.

Growing old is a journey
in different folks you can see
I never understood it all
till it started happening to me.

Now I've reached that time in life
that I dreaded one day would arrive
with declining health
daily I strive.

So that next time you see an old person
shake their hand now wrinkled and rough
try not to rush your life
you'll get there soon enough.

As a minister I am acutely aware of how swift life is,
like the weaver's shuttle it is fast.
In my own family, I have watched those grow old and depart
this life as it has declined for them quickly.
Age and sickness can bring a cruel decline of life,
unwelcome yet it comes.

James 4:14
Whereas ye know not what shall be on the morrow.
For what is your life?
It is even a vapour, that appeareth for a little time,
and then vanisheth away.

Running from God

*This man ran from God
after hearing him say
I need you to go here
he went another way.*

*He got on a boat
went down below
thinking that God
would never know.*

*Where he was going
or where he would be
all God needed
was a raging sea.*

*He pled for his cause
no one went his bail
in the depths of the sea
God prepared a whale.*

*To teach him a lesson
for running away
for that decision
Jonah would have to pay.*

*Jonah prayed aloud
said God, this is hell
for Jonah's rebellion
things were not going well.*

*God, if you'll get me
out of this mess
your name gladly
I will bless.*

The fish gave him up
on sandy dry ground
God spoke again
Jonah heard the sound.

He headed for Nineveh
with sermon in hand
to preach in the streets
and take God's stand.

For all this evil
I want to see
if he'll do to them
what he done to me.

God became angry
prepared a gourd and a worm
to teach man again
that his judgments are firm.

Then came the wind
that beat upon his head
by now Jonah
was wishing he was dead.

God said to Jonah
my anger is through
the city has repented
now I am finished with you.

For Jonah in all of this
it was for survival
but for God and cause
it was for revival.

THREE HEBREW CHILDREN

Three Hebrew children
in Daniel we are told
how they wouldn't bow
to the idols of gold.

Hearts filled with knowledge
wisdom and skill
no matter how tempted
they never lost the will.

To stand firm and anchored
in God's purpose and plan
dedicated to one God
never serve a man.

When you hear all kinds of music
you know what to do
bow down and worship
and the king will spare you.

But the three Hebrew children
acted as though
his decree that was sent out
they did not know.

They continued to stand
when given a second chance
in the fiery furnace
the king would get a glance.

Of how the God they served
would show his strong arm
they'd walk out of the furnace
with not one ounce of harm.

So they threw the men
in the furnace that day
those standing there
heard the king say.

I see four men
walking in there
the fire had not burned them
not even a hair.

The king was shaking
as he gave the nod
the fourth one I see
is like the son of God.

I hope you learn a lesson
from this poem I have written
that the Hebrew men's God
will deliver when you are smitten.

Remember this one thing
in the trial you are going through
God is still in the furnace
just to deliver you.

Now There Was a Day

Now there was a day
in the life of a man
enough bad things had happened
he could have ran.

He chose to stand
and not flee
even though he had lost
all his family.

Be true to God
and not get the blues
even after he had gotten
the awful bad news.

I serve you, God
not for what you do
it's not about doing
I simply love you.

Job lost everything
in a single day
not one time
did he ever say.

I curse you, God
for all the things you've done
I only did it
because I trust your son.

Job, you are my servant
there is no one like you
I'd never put more on you
that you can't go through.

I removed the hedge
and let Satan see
you would not sin
you were just like me.